AF464674

The Scarlet Thread

Doug M[c]Naught

Contact bekasume.books@optusnet.com.au

ISBN: 978-1-84753-409-5

Table of Contents

Preface

I am not a Hebrew expert. I just know enough to understand that there is a heavy aroma of grace hanging all over the entire Bible. Many people say that there is little or no grace in the Old Testament but I disagree. This book is written to give the reader the same sense of wonder that I have as I see the grace in the early part of the Bible. If we can establish the pattern of grace early in the Old Testament then we will see it throughout the remainder of the Scriptures.

If you want to talk an expert on Hebrew then talk to a Jew. They may disagree with me on some technical aspects but you can choose to see the grace or not.

How Safe Is My Rope?

Australia is said to be the driest continent on earth. Most of the rain falls around the coastal fringes, especially on the eastern coast. In the north, the monsoon rains come to make the summers wet but then the winters are long and dry. This means that the cattle stations in many parts of Australia are very large. In other countries they might be called cattle farms or ranches. Some of the stations are hundreds of square kilometres in area.

Apart from small areas around the homesteads, these stations are unfenced. The cattle roam freely throughout their range. This is not a problem because they stay near their own regular supply of water; sometimes walking many kilometres each day to go from their waterhole to their feeding grounds.

Greenhide

In spite of this, they grow the cattle to be sold as beef. Every year, musterers go from the stations to catch and brand the cattle. These days they take portable yards and muster the cattle using helicopters but, for many years, yards were built in the bush and the stockmen mustered the cattle on horseback.

During the process of mustering the stockmen need to use rope. Sometimes a bull would need to be tied up so that the cows would come more easily. The old scrub bulls could be very difficult and would, sometimes, try to gore the riders.

Ropes are made on the spot, using greenhide. (The Americans call this rawhide) A cow or steer would be killed and then the hide cleaned, the meat was also kept for feeding the stockmen. One of the musterers would cut the hide in a large spiral, starting from the middle. This makes a long strand of green leather. Three strands are taken and put on a rope-making machine. One on end the rope is attached to a heavy weight, which can slide along the ground. Each strand is twisted as tight as possible, all in the same direction. The weight keeps the strands taught. When this process is finished, the three strands are twisted together in the opposite direction. This means that as the strands try to unwind the twist the rope tighter and as the rope tries to unwind it twists the strands tighter. King Solomon spoke about this fact in Ecclesiastes 4:12 when he said that a cord made of three twisted strands is not easily broken.

Green hide ropes are stiff; they keep a loop open. The musterers know they can trust the ropes because they have made them. When the ropes get old and begin to rot the musterers can easily make more. They kill some of their beasts from time to time anyway, as they need to eat meat while they are working the cattle.

For the musterers, ropes play an important role in their job they would not be able to complete the task without them. Many other people rely on ropes as well but most people do not have the privilege of making their own ropes. We have to rely on ropes that other people make.

Can I Rely On My Rope?

There is a story told of a young man who tried to climb the Matterhorn, a mountain in Switzerland. He fell and his rope broke and was killed. When some men went out to find his body they discovered that he had been using the wrong kind of rope. A climbing rope is meant to be strong enough to hold a man when he falls but this rope broke. How can we know if a rope is designed for climbing?

In the days when this man fell to his death, all ropes were made of cotton or hemp. The strands were twisted and then three strands were twisted together in the same way as the green hide rope. But, how could a person know if the rope was of good enough quality to use as a lifeline while climbing? The same problem existed for sailors. They used ropes all the time and they would be in danger if their ropes broke.

Good quality ropes, which could sustain a fall, were always made with a scarlet thread running through the rope. Each strand was made with the scarlet thread on the outside. Anyone could tell when they looked at the rope that it was of sufficient quality to sustain a fall. Before the Second World War, all ropes used by the Royal Australian Navy had to have the scarlet thread.

Anyone who wanted to use a rope for a secure purpose, one that they could trust with their lives, could use a rope with the scarlet thread and be confident that it would hold when they needed.

Christians have a secure lifeline of their own. This lifeline is called the Bible; it is God's letter given to us so that we can know how to live today for God's glory and our good. We can tell that this lifeline is secure because it has a scarlet thread running through it. The scarlet thread is the thread of grace. As we open the Bible and begin to read the first verse we can see the scarlet thread of grace. This thread is visible as we read through every chapter. Romans 5:20 (NIV) tells us, "The law was added so that the trespass might increase. But where sin increased, grace increased all the more" As sin entered the world the grace of God shines out even more brightly.

A Heavy Aroma

I used to live in the far north west of Queensland in Australia. The dry country was cris-crossed by rivers. While much of the countryside was quite dry, the riverbanks always abounded with life. There were tall trees by the rivers and creeks with the roots drinking the water. Often the banks were crowded with ti trees; they were also called paperbark trees. During August and September these trees would be in flower and the heavy sweet smell of their flowers would almost be overpowering. As we walked along the river the sweet smell would fill our nostrils.

This is also true of the Bible: the sweet heavy aroma of grace is strong on every page. We can trust the Bible to be our life instructor because it is full of grace. The grace of God is the guarantee that it is secure and trustworthy. If we ask the Holy Spirit to open our eyes we will see the grace on every page and we will, consequently, be able to see the grace in every day of our lives.

This purpose of this book is to look at God's grace in the Bible. We will not look at every page; that would take an entire lifetime of study. A quick look at some of the early passages will show the pattern and we will rejoice in the truth of Romans 5:20 as well.

Culture

At Doomadgee State School the students studied culture every week. This was just as important as learning the three R's. Some old men and women would come to the school from the "camp" to teach the younger girls and boys. The children needed to know who they were and where they came from so that they would understand their place in society. I won't mention any names at this stage, as it is not proper to mention the name of any deceased person in Aboriginal culture. These older people had been born and spent their childhoods in the bush so they knew most of the details of their culture. Sometimes the children would be taken out into the bush and learn how to find or hunt for food. At other times they would be taught how to track animals and where to find them.

Cultural Guidelines

Many of the lessons were devoted to telling the children stories. There were different kinds of stories for different occasions. Some stories were told to the younger children while others were for the initiated men or women. The non-Aboriginal schoolteachers were allowed to hear the general stories but only initiated people were told their stories. The children grew up with their mothers at first and learnt to speak the women's language. As boys grew older they were moved away from the women's domain and had to learn a men's language. Later they would also learn an initiated language. Some men would be able to speak three languages to communicate in different areas of their lives. The women also had their own initiated language.

These people did have some form of written language to allow them to communicate between the clans. Sometimes they would leave pictorial messages on the walls of caves or rock overhangs to remind other people of their history while at other times the messages were just simple ways of passing information from one group to another.

However, most of their history was committed to memory. The children would be told the stories many times and then they would have to repeat them until they were word perfect. In a society where there are no books or electronic form of communication their entertainment comes from telling stories or having corroborees. The corroborees are acted out to tell stories as well. There are different kinds of corroborees; some are just for entertainment and tell stories from the past while others are only for the initiated.

At the end of a hard day the clan or family group would sit together and eat their food. After this they would settle around the fire and someone would begin to tell stories. Everyone would be happy to hear about the heroes of times past and their great deeds. The process of story telling would also keep the group together and maintain their shared struggle for survival in the harsh land.

The children had to learn many things; they needed to know how to keep the balance of nature and not kill out any kind of plant or animal. They would learn their "skin group" so that the tribe could continue to survive without losing genetic diversity or becoming inbred. There were at least four different skin groupings and people from one skin grouping could only marry people from one other skin grouping.

Each person also belonged to a particular "dreaming". These subgroups gave people responsibility over certain plants or animals, they were also allowed to hunt or gather these plants or animals. In this way the biodiversity of the local ecosystem was preserved without too much pressure being placed on any kind of plant or animal.

Stories

All this information is told as a series of stories. Each particular piece of information is attached to a story and the story is repeated often so that the children will learn the information.

These stories also give the young people a context and a reason for acting according to the rules of their society. There is never a question as to why they should or should not participate in a particular kind of behaviour. While they may not understand the subtleties of inbreeding or the dictates of biodiversity within their ecological context they do know what is right and what is wrong so that these pressures don't force the destruction of their habitat or clan.

As a person grows older they may understand the more complicated reasons behind their cultural dictates but at first they only know the stories. However, as long as they know the stories then all the other obligations are met as well.

The main point to understand is that these stories answer the interrogatives: "why", "where", "how", "who" and "what". In a more fractured society these interrogatives still have to be answered. Children are sent to designated places of learning so that the will learn the answers. This is really no different to a unified culture where the storyteller teaches rather than a qualified teacher.

Toledoth

Ancient clay tablets found in Mesopotamia all have a similar structure. A Toledoth is placed at the end of any series of tablets. Toledoth is a Hebrew word meaning "generations", "origins" or "histories". An ancient author would place his qualifications and pedigree at the end of his tablet. This would add authenticity to the tablet and allow any readers living at the time to check his credentials to write the document.

The fact that the book of Genesis contains eleven Toledoth (2: 4; 5: 1; 6: 9; 10: 1; 11: 10; 11: 27; 25: 12, 19; 36: 1, 9: 37: 2) shows that it is a very ancient book. Using these Toledoth we can see that Genesis can be divided up into nine sections:

Genesis 1: 1-2: 4 ends with "These are the generations of the heavens and of the earth when they were created, in the day that the LORD God made the heavens and the earth". This means that this is the first section and is a very ancient document[i] indeed. Who but God could have written this section because he was the only witness to these events? This theory has Biblical support because we know from Exodus 24: 12; 32:16 that God wrote the original tablets that contained the Law with his own finger.

The next section Genesis 2: 5-5: 2 is Adam's document. Looking at this section from this point of view we can see that there is no conflict between the, so called, "two accounts" of creation. One is written from God's point of view and the other is written from Adam's point of view.

The rest of the sections are: the book of Noah (5: 3-6:9a); the book of the sons of Noah (6: 9b-10: 1a); the book of Shem (10: 1b-11: 10a); the book of Terah (11: 10b-27a), the book of Isaac and Ishmael (11: 27b-25: 19a); the book of Jacob and Esau (25: 19b-37: 2a); the book of the sons of Jacob (Gen 37: 2b-Ex 1: 4). This last book is in a slightly different form because it was constructed in Egypt and used their style rather than the older style from Mesopotamia.

Alienation

When a person is alienated from their genetic heritage at birth they often have a hunger to find their anchors because every one wants to answer the interrogatives. An adopted child brought up in a loving and emotionally rich environment will still long to find out about their biological heritage when they reach adulthood. The Australians of the "Stolen Generations" may have been separated from their heritage with good intentions and some were even given a compassionate upbringing but they all felt a sense of alienation from their roots.

In our post-modern society we no longer understand the importance of grandparents. A child's parents teach them the immediate imperatives of the present and the future so that they can survive and prosper. Grandparents should be teaching the children the less pressing imperatives of the past so that they know who they are and can establish an anchor for their souls. In the final analysis a child must be prepared for the present and the future but they can only do this on a firm foundation of the past.

Sometimes a child will be given more than one story to illustrate a particular point in their heritage. These stories are never contradictory; rather they illustrate different aspects or emphases concerning that part of their culture. With the extra information the child will know how to act under different circumstances according to their own place in the society.

Vision Statement

Most companies have a vision statement today. This vision statement is placed prominently wherever the company conducts its business. If a person joins the company they will be given some kind of induction seminar so that they know how to behave and what role they have.

But why do they have a vision statement? The vision statement empowers every individual in the company, whatever their level, to make decisions. A neophyte will be told to learn the vision statement of the company and this will tell them what the company plans to do as it goes about its business. When a person has a decision to make, within their role and authority, they will automatically look at the vision statement and decide which course of action will further the company's vision.

This is even truer of an entire culture. Children are taught their place and their cultural aspirations in the context of the stories. When they are older and in a position to make decisions they will know what is expected of them and will be able to decide accordingly.

Two Scenarios

Scenario A

Many scholars today say that the majority of the Old Testament was written during the time of the Exile. They say that the Old Testament is the product of a conflict between: the Northern and the Southern tribes of Israel; the people who came into the Promised Land via Kadesh and those who came in over the Jordan River; the people who know God as "Elohim" and the people who know God as "Jahweh"; the people who believe that the Law was given at Horeb and those who believe that the Law was given at Sinai; the people who believe that the Lord chose Shechem as the place for central worship and those who believe that the Lord

Jerusalem as the place for central worship. This conflict leads to the use of various names for God in different stories.

The Old Testament was built up over time with redactors from the various schools adding and adapting parts of the story to show that their point of view was the correct one. At a later date a group of priestly editors took the text and adapted it again so that they would enshrine the importance of their own role in Holy Scripture.

Under this scenario the Old Testament becomes a book that is really untrustworthy. When we read the final text, as we have it, we can only examine it carefully to find the sources and then we can assume that they were writing to serve their own purpose rather than tell the story as it actually happened.

This scenario leads to some problems; if a person tells us lies when they introduce themselves to us then we won't be able to trust them on any issue after that. If God tells us lies when he first introduces himself to us then we can't trust God at any stage.

Scenario B

If we believe that things are the same today as they have always been, we can assume that Abraham belonged to a complex and highly structured culture like the one at Doomadgee. When he was a child he was given the stories by some of the older people just like the young people today. However there were some differences; Adam[ii] was still alive when Lamech was born. Lamech was still alive when Shem was born and Shem was still alive when Abram was born. Abraham also had copies of the ancient tablets that had been handed down by his family from the beginning.

While Abraham didn't produce his own tablet the record of his life was included in the book of Isaac and Ishmael.

Neither Adam nor Lamech knew that the world was going to be flooded at a later date. They were, however, just like modern humans and were deeply concerned that their young people would know their heritage[iii]. By the time Lamech was born, Adam was telling the stories to children about his younger days. He was only interested in giving them the stories that answered the interrogatives rather than the stories that a modern historian or scientist might record. When young Shem learned the stories he was taught them without being given any knowledge of the Flood because it hadn't happened and no one knew that it would. Not only did they have the stories they also had the tablets that were written before the Flood.

As an old man, Shem still told the stories to his descendants and handed on his collection of clay tablets. He was a treasured resource because of his great age and the fact that he had close contact with the very first man; Shem was only separated from Creation by one generational memory. He was true to the stories that he was taught and taught them to Abram as he had learnt them.

Because each story was significant he made sure that he didn't deviate from words that Lamech had told him he could also check these stories against his clay tablets. Sometimes he would use the Name "Elohim" because that story was important in teaching about the fact that God is Almighty and at other times he would use the Name "Jahweh" because that story was important in teaching about God's relationship blessings for his people.

Each generation also has to add some stories so that the next generation of children will have a complete record of their culture and the place of each individual in that culture. From time to time extra tablets were added to the collection as well. Adam started with his stories; Seth learned those stories till they were word perfect to the clay tablet then he added some to include his own history and so on.

Terah left his place at Ur, and headed away with his son Abram to Haran. From this point on Abram (soon to become Abraham) started adding his own stories but things were different now because God had spoken to Abram in a personal way and Abram believed God.

Moses

If we move forward in history to the time of Moses we find that Pharaoh's daughter adopted him[iv]. Even though Moses was adopted into the royal family, he needed a wet nurse to satisfy his early hunger. Children learn a vast amount of information as to their culture and their heritage while they are learning to speak. A child's mother always has a profound influence on their thinking throughout their life.

His Hebrew mother brought up Moses until the time that he was weaned. Jochebed was a slave in Egypt but she was also a loyal Hebrew because she kept her son alive even though Pharaoh had commanded that every Hebrew baby boy be killed at birth. As Moses learned to talk his mother told him the stories that she had heard while she was growing up.

While it is true that the Hebrews were slaves, they still had some time at the end of the day where they would eat and spend time together before sleeping. By the time that Moses was taken away from his mother and trained in Pharaoh's household he was been taught the stories that had come all the way down from Adam.

Moses lived in Pharaoh's palace until he was forced to run away to a foreign country when he acted foolishly. Later he returned to Egypt after meeting God in the desert and led Israel out of slavery. When these people came out of slavery they knew some of the stories but they needed to know more. Why did they spend four hundred years as slaves? Why did God intervene in a miraculous way to set them free?

When the immediate danger of recapture was removed God took his people to Mount Sinai in Horeb district and gave them the answers to their interrogatives. Moses, as the leader, was in control of the ancient history as written on the clay tablets.

"All Scripture is inspired by God and profitable for teaching, for reproof, for correction, for training in righteousness; so that the man of God may be adequate, equipped for every good work." (2 Timothy 3:16, 17 (NASB95)[v].)

God used the information that Moses had learned while he was still very young from his mother and the clay tablets as the basis for the inspired answers to the interrogatives. Moses himself was able to add to these stories to complete the history of his own life and then someone, maybe Joshua, added the last chapter of Moses' life; discussing his death and burial.

The Butcher and the Anatomist

But what does modern research tell us about the Bible? Where do these ideas come from? It is interesting to study the history of modern Biblical criticism and see when and how their ideas developed.

The Butcher and the Anatomist

The Australian philosopher Gavin Ardley said that there are two ways of analysing or dissecting something: We can follow the process of the anatomist and carefully examine the structure or we can be like a butcher who is not concerned with the structure of the animal. The anatomist wants to find the structure while the butcher wants to cut the meat so that it can be eaten so he makes his own structure.

When we look at the Bible we can try to find the structure by whatever means we have at our disposal or we can try to force the documents into a structure that best fits our purposes.[vi]

Scientific Biblical Criticism

The first person to look at the Old Testament documents in a scientific way was a French Priest called Richard Simon (1638-1712)[vii] who became the forerunner of modern Biblical Criticism. His work didn't survive for long, however, Jean Astruc in 1753 published a book that looked at the different names used for God in the early part of the Bible and said that Moses had joined two pre-existing documents together. Following him Gottfried Eichhorn in his Introduction to the Old Testament (1780-83) carefully analysed the Pentateuch and developed the "fragment hypothesis". He showed that part of the Pentateuch documents were written by Moses but the rest was put together later.

Another scholar called De Wette began the theory known as historical criticism. He used evidence from vocabulary and style as well as arguments drawn from history to show that the Pentateuch was made up of legend and poetry.

We can critically divide books by examining the words and the style that the writer uses and the fact that some narratives are repeated from different viewpoints.

Cuneiform Writing

In 1835 a British army officer serving in Persia found the Behistun inscriptions. This officer was called Henry Rawlinson[viii]. This inscription was carved in the three official languages of King Darius of Persia's Empire. Rawlinson along with another man called Edward Hincks set out to interpret these texts. Later a panel of experts examined their translations as well as those of Julius Oppert and William Henry Fox Talbot to say that the Akkadian cuneiform was now understood.

Archaeology

As a modern science the study of archaeology is only about 150 years old[ix]. Of course for thousands of years people have been digging up graves and similar monuments for various reasons. There is a tradition that Nabonidus, who was the last king of the Neo Babylonian Empire performed and archaeological dig. Belshazzar, the king of Daniel 6 was only acting as regent for his father Nabonidus who was living on an oasis in the desert.

In the seventeenth and eighteenth centuries enlightened scholars looked into sites in Ancient Greece to see where rationalism came from. They believed that rationalism was the supreme human reason. In the 1840s an Englishman called Austen Henry Layard searched for and found ancient Nineveh. Rawlinson was also involved in archaeological research in Persia.

Without the Benefit

From this short history we can see that the field of modern Biblical criticism was developed without the benefit of modern archaeology or an understanding of the language of the cuneiform tablets.

Grace

There is an old rhyme that goes like this: "Patience is a virtue, virtue is a grace, and Grace is a little girl who doesn't wash her face." We have to stop and ask ourselves what grace really is. Is it just one of those technical Christian words that we use but don't understand or is it really important? John Newton, the man who wrote "Amazing Grace" one of the most popular songs of the second millennium, believed that there was something special about grace; it gave him the motivation to write his great hymn.

An old acronym has been used many times to explain grace: God's Riches At Christ's Expense. This is a good explanation but how can we talk about Christ when we are reading the Old Testament? We will examine this question later.

A simple way to distinguish between grace and mercy will give the best idea. Grace occurs when we get something that we don't deserve while mercy occurs when we don't get something that we do deserve.

Old Testament Grace

One of the best places to look for information on Old Testament words is "The Theological Wordbook of the Old Testament[x]." When we look at the Old Testament word for "grace" we can see that it comes from the idea of pity or begging. There is also an idea of being given something that we don't deserve. Sometimes a person will see that someone else is in trouble and they will feel compassion for them and do something to help. This kind of activity only goes one way, from a superior person to an inferior person, or from a person in a stronger position to a person in a weaker position. This idea, superior and inferior, doesn't occur much in the modern democratic concept but in older times people were born with status and were able to give favour to a person who didn't have so much status. It was almost impossible for a person to move from one level of status to another level of status without an application of grace.

There also seems to be an indication of loyalty on the part of the superior person. Someone is under the influence or control of a superior person and that superior person takes this influence or control seriously. In the social situation a person who controlled other people had certain obligations to them. This idea of obligation is absent when we consider God and the fact that he owes nothing to any person.

Grace

It is always a good idea to see how Old Testament scholars of a previous age looked at words. Some time between 300 and 200 BC Jewish scholars translated the Hebrew Old Testament into a Greek version[xi]. There were many Jews who spoke Greek at that time and many non-Jews were interested as well.

At that time the Hebrew scholars chose Greek words that meant "to have compassion" or "show mercy" or "plead". There was no hint of any obligation on the part of the superior person from these scholars. There are always poor and needy people but they cannot force those who are not to do anything for them; when help comes it comes as a surprise and should be accepted with gratitude.

Even though this word applies to people of superior rank it usually applies to God. In the Psalms, the writer pleads with God to show him grace when he is suffering or lonely. The Lord is sovereign and he does whatever he wants to do[xii]. No one can force him to change his attitude or his decisions; however, the Lord only does good things[xiii] but he is under no obligation to do good for any particular person[xiv]. Every time God deals with an individual or a group of people he deals in grace.

In some cases people use the idea of grace when they are asking God for something. Even though Moses was told that he would not be able to go into the Promised Land, he begged the Lord to let him go into the Land[xv] but Lord allowed him to look over the River and see the Land from a distance. This demonstrates God's grace in that he allows people to ask him to show his grace by dealing with them.

Sometimes the idea of grace has a thought of someone finding favour in another person's opinion. When Ruth came to visit Boaz she prayed that she would find favour in his eyes[xvi].

The idea of grace is also expanded to include someone doing something for no reason. In some circumstances this may be something bad happening for no reason but also good things happen to people who, seemingly, don't deserve them. Saul persecuted David for no reason, before he became king. Saul had a reason for persecuting David because he was afraid of David but David hadn't done anything to make King Saul want to destroy him. God doesn't have to have a reason to do good for any person other than the fact that God is good. No one has something that will impress God enough for him to want to be good to him or her. God has no ulterior motive when he is good to us because we don't have the resources to offer him anything valuable in return.

New Testament Grace

The New Testament writers, except Luke, were all Jews and their heart languages were Aramaic and Hebrew. They most probably, as all good Jews, learnt the Scripture from the early years and thought in Hebrew. Their understanding of Grace was heavily influenced by their Old Testament studies. Much of the information about Grace from the Old Testament is relevant to the New Testament concept of "grace" because most of the New Testament writers had a strong Jewish background[xvii].

Greek writers, outside the New Testament took the word to mean, variously; "something that delights or causes pleasure", or "something that caused joy", it could also mean an act of favour that was shown and received or given in kindness. Grace developed in meaning with time to mean favour shown by a ruler. Grace can also mean “power that has come down from the gods” so it has a religious connotation as well.

In the New Testament “grace” is associated with the message of the gospel. Grace occurs when someone is delighted by a gift or being given something they haven’t earned and don’t deserve.

In The Beginning

Read- Genesis 1:1

In Hebrew the Bible begins with two words that we translate as "In the beginning" and "created". Both these words have the letters that we might write as "BRA"[xviii] this indicates that they are related. In fact, the word "beginning" implies "creation" and the word "creation" implies "beginning" we can't have one without the other. The connection between these two words is important because many people today say that they are many other ways that the world began but not according to the Bible.

A New Start

Scientists today, talk about a "Big Bang". They say that the world began with a big bang when our time started. The big bang was so intense that any evidence of what happened before the bang was destroyed. The Bible teaches us that there was nothing before the first moment of creation. The Lord started our world and our time from the beginning. He didn't use the remains of some previous, failed universe. It is good to know that God was gracious when he created the world, he stared a new world and everything was fresh.

"For you created my inmost being; you knit me together in my mother's womb. I praise you because I am fearfully and wonderfully made; your works are wonderful, I know that full well." (Psalm 139: 13:14: (NIV)) tells us that this is true for each person as well. We only have one existence and we don't have to worry about sins committed by another person in another lifetime.

The world God made has no residue of evil from another time or another race of people. We are not responsible for the misdeeds of people we don't know. This establishes a principle that is spoken about in Ezekiel 18:4 (The soul who sins is the one who will die. (NIV)). Everyone is responsible for his or her own destiny. If we have to rely on someone else then we are helpless but if we are responsible for our own destiny then we can do something about the situation. God is gracious to give each person a new beginning.

People who believe that we have previous lives place a huge weight on the shoulders of every baby that is born. A human baby is the most helpless being on earth but they expect each baby to carry the burden of someone else's sins before they have done anything themselves. Individually and as the human race we don't have to bear any burdens that other people have made for us.

Only God

The word "created" implies two important points. This word only ever has God as its subject. The only other type of "creation" means, "made from other raw materials." When God creates, he makes something from nothing without using other raw materials. Later we have God making man out of the dust of the earth but this is not an act of creation in the same sense.

God, in his grace, is involved in the process. He doesn't send someone else to do this job. Had God sent another being to do this job then there would be problems. The other being would always lust after God's position. There would a power struggle. We would have a situation where we would not know who to obey and who to love. God did not create this kind of tension into the world that he made for us.

The first verse of the Bible establishes an important principle: when God does the really important things, he does them himself. God never relies on another person or being to do the big things. That way God knows that the important things are done properly. There is never a chance of something going astray in the process. God's grace is such that he is willing to give us every chance of getting the best out of whatever he makes without any outside interference.

The act of creation also implies that God was able to create with absolute ease. There was no struggle! Many other religions teach that there was a great struggle in the process of creation and that is why there is evil in the world. Evil was a by-product of struggle. Someone, somewhere wasn't able to cope with the task they had been given and then evil was produced. The Bible has God independent of evil in every way. There is no possibility of God producing evil or losing control so that evil had a victory.

God creates without any struggle, he creates perfectly and he is always in complete control. If we were to assume that God's control was less than absolute we would sink into a position where we could never have absolute security. Life would then be reduced to "luck". Our eternal destiny would no longer be guaranteed by God's absolute power it would become arbitrary and random.

When God finished creating the world, there was no sweat on his Divine brow. He knew exactly where everything was and he had control over everything. We see a universe, which defies our human minds it is so great but God is far greater than the entire universe. He knows where every subatomic particle is at every moment of time (see Colossians 1:18). Not only that, he has told every subatomic particle where it should be. Our God controls everything with an iron control and nothing escapes that control. Before the world began our God had every moment of time planned to the last detail. Imagine having a God that was less than that. If an event took God by surprise we would have no guarantees about anything.

Who is this God?

Who is this God? The word "God" means "Mighty One"[xix]. It is impossible to know God in the sense that we can have control over him in any way. God is beyond all our imagination let alone our ability to control his reactions. God is God and there is no one else like him in the entire universe. He is in a league of his own.

In 1 Kings 20, we have the story of Ben Hadad, king of the Arameans, fighting against Israel. He was soundly defeated but managed to escape from the battlefield. In verse 23 of that chapter the king's officials tell him that the God of Israel is a God of the hills and all they have to do is fight against Israel on the plains and they will win. This is typical of their beliefs; they believed that if they knew enough about God then they could defeat him. Of course they were wrong and suffered another great defeat on the plains.

This is why it is so important that our God cannot be known. His name just means "Mighty One". There is nothing to "know" about a God like that. This kind of God can never be defeated, he is always more powerful than anyone who tries to conquer him.

In Particular

The words "God created the heavens" mean that God created everything. Wherever we can look we see things that God made and we can never see anything that is outside God's creation. All the buildings and other structures made by man are just made out of resources that were created by God. God makes the wonderful things modern man uses including the minds, which invented them.

Why does the fist verse include the words "and the earth"? If God made everything why do we have to know that he made the earth? Surely the earth is part of everything? The sense of this verse is that while God made everything, he made the earth in particular. At the time when everything began, God already set the earth apart as a special place for a special purpose. God planned to do something with the earth that was different to anything else in the universe that he had made.

The grace of God shines through this verse in many ways. In comparison to our solar system the earth is insignificant. If we place our solar system next to the Milky Way Galaxy then our solar system is insignificant. But, there are many thousands of galaxies in the universe and the Milky Way is only insignificant among those giant galaxies. It seems as though there is nothing more insignificant than the earth but God set the earth apart for something special.

If we look at one individual person among the 6.3 billion people who make up the earth we can see that one person is insignificant. If we put every person on earth in the Mariana Trench, the deepest part of the oceans, they would all fit there and have less effect on the level of the oceans than would the melting of the polar ice cap. If we try to compare one person with God we can see how insignificant we are in the whole scheme of things.

In spite of this, we are created in God's image and are able to have a relationship with him. God has done this on purpose to make us humble. We are not made to be humble so that we will feel bad about ourselves but so that we will feel good about God. What a privilege to have an "in particular" relationship with the Lord and Creator of the universe.

Who, Why, How?

The nation of Israel spent about four hundred years as slaves in Egypt (see Genesis 15:13). When they came out of slavery they needed to know whom they were, why they were here and how they were going to survive. The years they spent in Egypt as slaves were important years. Abraham had two sons and there was strife between the two sons. To this very day the strife between Arab and Israeli continues. Isaac had two sons and they fought for most of their lives. They continued to fight with each other over many years until the descendants of Esau disappeared from history as prophesied by Jeremiah. (Jeremiah 49:17, 18) It seems as though the descendants of Old Testament brothers were destined to fight.

On the other hand, the children of Israel came from a family at war. The two wives were two sisters who fought each other as rivals. Their father set up this by giving the older sister to Jacob when he loved and wanted her younger sister. To make matters worse, Rachel, the preferred wife didn't have any children for a long time. She gave her personal slave to her husband to have children on her behalf. In response to this, Leah also gave her personal slave to her husband. This was a recipe for disaster but throughout the centuries the descendants of Jacob have formed the nation of Israel that still exists today.

The reason they have stayed together, even beyond the time when they became two nations, was that their national identity was forged while they were slaves in Egypt. When this time of slavery ended the Israelis were a nation of slaves and they did not understand their role before God.

Moses, their leader spent forty days in conference with the Lord on the top of Mt Sinai (Exodus 24: 18). During this time God gave Moses the answers to the above questions as well as other important information. The nation of slaves needed to know how they were to behave. God chose them as his special, "in particular" people and there was a responsibility for them to live up to that high calling. The first verse of the Bible answers the "Who?", "How?", "Why?" questions. Israel was set apart "in particular" to be the recipients of God's grace. Of course, the promise God made to Abram widened the "in particular" aspect to all the families of the earth. (Genesis 12: 1-3) The people of the earth were set apart by God to belong to him so that he could give the earth to us to own as his stewards.

We make a big mistake if we treat Genesis as a scientific textbook in the modern sense of the word. It was not designed to be that kind of book. The Bible is a relationship book designed for God's "in particular" people to know more about God so that we can enjoy all the benefits of our "in particular" relationship with God.

Generosity

Creation is actually God's first generous act. He did not have to make us but he freely chose to make us anyway. Next to

God the entire universe is small and insignificant so we are even more insignificant (Compare Deuteronomy 7: 7). In spite of this, God made the earth "in particular" so that we could enjoy God's love. We were made in God's image so that we could have a relationship with God. This is another act of grace on God's part.

The whole of the first verse of the Bible has a heavy aroma of grace. By the grace of God and the power of the Holy Spirit we can see and enjoy the love of God and his grace in making us to enjoy his love. The whole of creation is there so that we can be amazed at God's power and majesty. We can see the stars at night or the wonder of God's creation by day and be drawn to a deep sense of amazement at the greatness of his grace.

And God Said

Read- Genesis 1:2-31

If Genesis 1:1 gives us the story of how God made the world, why do we have the rest of the chapter? There are experts who talk about the Gap theory here. They say that there is a Gap between verses one and two. That Gap allows people to put just about anything they want in the Gap. This may the place where Satan sinned but that leads to problems as well. Why did God see that everything was very good if Satan sinned at this stage surely he would have seen sin and not everything as very good?

The Gap

Some people say that is when evolution happened. Others say that the Gap makes the world old because it took many millions of years. Another group say that there is just a small Gap when Satan sinned so there was sin in the world before God began to create.

Perhaps we can look elsewhere to see if there is some other explanation. A good example to consider is Psalm 23 (NIV). It begins with a statement, "The Lord is my Shepherd, and I shall lack nothing." This introduction is followed by an exposition of that statement. The rest of the Psalm just tells us what it means to have the Lord as our Shepherd. It is not just enough to know that the Lord is our Shepherd; we are told how this will affect our lives as well.

The book of Mark, in the New Testament, begins with an introduction as well, "The beginning of the Gospel of Jesus Christ, the Son of God." That introduction is followed by a long explanation of how the Gospel of Jesus Christ came into being. There would be no gospel without the Lord Jesus Christ and his earthly life, followed by his death and resurrection.

Genesis 1:1 gives us the statement, "In the beginning God created the heavens and the earth." After this we have an explanation of how God went about this task. There is no need to assume that there has to be a Gap. God begins his story of creation with the fact that he made the heavens and the earth then he goes on to explain how he did this wonderful act of generosity and grace.

We don't have to worry about anything; God is in control. He has targeted us to enjoy his love, to appreciate his grace and to be amazed at his glory.

And God Said

Genesis 1 is dominated by the majesty of God, he speaks and things happen. God is the only Person who can speak and guarantee that something will happen. In a day when people are told that they can determine every outcome in their lives it is good to see that God is in control.

Some years ago my father asked me to come to his house and seal his bathroom window. The bathroom was on the second floor and it was too high for him to work there as he was quite sick at the time. He bought a long ladder to do the job and told me that when I finished the job he would give me the ladder. I went to his house and put lead flashing around the window so that it no longer leaked in the rain.

Later, I took the ladder home and leant it to a friend who needed the ladder. About a year later my mother asked me where her ladder was and demanded that I bring it back to her. The situation should have been easy to solve, all we had to do was ask my father what he said about the ladder. The issue was complicated because he had died in the intervening period.

My father made a promise to me but he could not make sure that his promise was kept because he was no longer alive. This illustrates the importance of the words, "And God said," He is the only Person who will not die. The Lord Jesus Christ was dead for three days but he rose again and is alive now. He will never die again.

God speaks and his word remains fixed. He will never die. Even the greatest lawyer in the world cannot find a way to force God to change his word. Throughout the Old Testament we have examples of God speaking and then his word being kept.

In Jeremiah 1: 12 (NIV), the Lord says, "I am watching to see that my word is fulfilled." God is involved in the process himself and he has the authority to make decisions. When he makes a promise, he always keeps because no one has the authority to change his decisions.

When God speaks the result it always the same, "It was so." There is an immediate response to God's spoken word. Whatever God commands, happens. When David wished for water while he was in the cave of Adullam (2 Samuel 23:14), his soldiers heard his wish and they risked their lives to get that water. Creation hears the slightest wish of the Creator and it rushes to obey that wish.

Not only does Creation obey God's command but also the things that God commands are good. Genesis 1:31 (NIV), "God saw all the he had made and it was very good." The grace of God flows uninhibited throughout this chapter. He creates by his own divine grace and everything is good. There is no sin in the world when God finishes creating. He has created a perfect world so that his creatures can know his goodness.

There is no room for sin at this stage. God saw everything that he had made and it was good. He made the angels (see Psalm

104: 4) but when he looked at everything he had made it was good. Some people say that there was sin at this stage but sin came later.

Evening and Morning

God was able to create the entire universe and everything in it with one great command but he took his time. We read that there was evening and morning, in all, a total of six days on which God commanded things and they happened.

God is infinite and divine while we are finite and temporal. We are very small when compared with God and no human has the capacity to know all there to know about God. We are only able to know the few, small things that he tells us about himself. The earth is a finite, temporal representation of God's divine majesty. He has done this so that we can understand something about him and then enjoy his goodness.

Our minds are only able to understand things slowly; we have to build our understanding of facts that we have already learnt. A baby comes into the world and takes time to learn how to speak, walk and read. If we had all the information as soon as we were born we would be overwhelmed and would never really appreciate everything that we knew.

In Exodus 23: 29-33, the Lord is talking to Israel about the land that he has promised to give them. He told them that he would give the land to them slowly. Little by little their enemies would be chased out of the land. Why would God do this? Wouldn't it be easier to give them the whole land without any struggle so that they just get what was promised?

The Lord was concerned that the land would turn into a desert because there was no one to look after it. While Israel was conquering the land, the people there would look after all the parts that they hadn't conquered and the land would be looked after. Wild animals will quickly take over a place where there are no people and they would have to fight the wild animals to possess the land.

While God doesn't have to take his time doing things, we do. We are restricted by our humanity. God's grace is seen in the fact that he took time to create the earth. The earth was made so that we could possess it but we don't have the capacity to do anything in a hurry. God set this pattern for our good. His grace was sufficient to see our needs and to satisfy them. A less than gracious God would have done his own thing and not taken the time to look after our human weakness.

If we have to work for something we appreciate it much better than if we don't have to work for it. God took his time to make the world in six days for our benefit.

Everything Was Very Good

It seems as though God began by creating the matter and energy that was needed for the universe then he began to mould it and form the bodies, as we know them today. He begins with light. "And God said, 'Let there be light and there was light.'" The basic condition for life is the presence of light. There is more light than we need.

God's grace is the same. There is always more than enough and it is best used and passed on. Nothing is wasted in

God's plan. When the animals are finished with their energy and matter they are recycled through the system continuously. Not only does God create light but he separated light from darkness.

Everybody needs rest so that they can live. God makes sure that we have time to repair and recuperate during our lives. The idea of light coming first looks forward to the time mentioned in John 1: 4 (NIV) "In him was life, and that life was the light of the world." Light and life are inseparable. This light also has the hint of the future light of regeneration. 2 Corinthians 4:16 has this sense, "But God, having said light from darkness shined forth, has shined light in out hearts." Light and life are partners but God gives spiritual life from spiritual light as well. As the light comes forth by God's grace so the light of salvation comes forth by God's grace.

The first three days cannot be solar days, as we know them. The sun and moon were not created until the fourth day.

The second day is a day of separation. The water beneath the earth was separated from the water above the earth. Before the flood there was no rain, this means that the earth was watered from the water that was stored in the sky. On the third day God divided the water on the earth into oceans, seas and rivers and separated the land. After this God put vegetation on the earth. We need to remember this is not written as a modern scientific treatise. It is a message from God, revealing his grace in creation. God tells his people what they need to know about how the earth was made and where the plants they eat came from. The whole of this narrative concentrates on the earth

Day four and God makes, rather than creates, the sun and the moon. The separation of light and darkness continues. There is an overriding clause; the light is able to conquer the darkness. Even in the darkness, the moon is able to shine. That heavenly body has no light of its own; it only has reflected light. If a person goes to place where there is no electric light he can see his way at night when there is no moon because there is a glow from the stars of the Milky Way Galaxy. Even in days of great sin, godly men and women are able to communicate with God and reflect his light on the world.

Every living being on earth ultimately gets its energy to live from the sun. Less than a billionth of the light produced by the sun lands on the earth but there is still enough to feed the earth. At the bottom of the food chains, plants capture the energy from the sun, via photosynthesis, and store it as energy. As we move up the food chain animals or plants either eat other plants or other animals that have eaten plants. This happened before sin came into the world but sin did not take God by surprise. He had already made plans to deal with sin's effects and maintain contact with the earth.

On the fifth day, God created the fish and birds. They were given the brief to multiply and fill the earth. The earth was made to be filled and there were enough resources on the earth the supply all these living creatures. The sixth day saw the introduction of the land animals, domestic and wild

Finally, after everything else was made, God made man in his own image. We were made to have a relationship with God and to enjoy his goodness.

God did not make the heavens and the earth for his own benefit. He was complete in every way before he created the heavens and the earth. He didn't need anything at all. However, God knew that if he made man in his own image and gave him a finite, tangible expression of his grace then man could enjoy God's goodness. God is gracious because he has made everything for our good and our enjoyment. Already the river of grace is in flood.

Rest

Read- Genesis 2: 1-3

After the six days of creation, God rested. We have been talking about how God was able to create with ease. There was no sweat on his Divine brow at the end of the first day of creation and this was true of every other day of creation. Why did God need to rest if he wasn't tired? God rested because there was nothing left to do. He had finished creating the world. He looked at everything that he had created and it was very good. This is the rest that every person longs for.

The Seventh Day

There is a human tendency to fix things even though there is nothing wrong with them. Every few years governments change and they change the way our countries operate. Things just seem to get worse at times but the need to fix them is still there. Big companies want people to keep buying their products so they make them with a limited life. God is gracious; he wants us to be secure in his consistency. When creation was finished, God didn't keep trying to fix it; he left things as they were so that man, and all the other creatures he had made, could have a secure world.

This establishes a principle of grace that runs throughout the entire Bible, God's rest is not a rest of exhaustion; it is a rest of completion. Whenever God is involved in humanity, his purpose is to make things complete.

Mathematicians talk about closure. There are certain conditions that make a system complete and one of these is closure. If you an apply operation to a system and the result remains within the system then we have closure. God has applied closure to his creation; this is the rest of completion. It is possible for people, inside their relationship with God, to be completely satisfied. Another blaze of grace illuminates the narrative.

This shows that God's plan is for us to be complete in him. We are made to give glory to God. We give glory to God when we enjoy all the good things he has for us. We cannot do anything to improve God's situation. He made us because he enjoys giving. Every time we accept that he is complete, and we rest in his completeness, we give him glory and we rest.

The idea of rest also contains the concept of covering over. A synonym for this kind of rest has something settling down on and wrapping itself around another object. In Isaiah 25:10 the hand of God rested upon the mountains. When God had finished creating, his spirit rested on the whole of creation. He stopped creating because there was nothing left to create but he did not leave creation alone. By contrast, in Genesis 1:2 the Spirit of God hovered over the waters.

God Blessed the Seventh Day

While it is true that God created man in his own image, we can see that the seventh day is the jewel in the crown of creation. God gave man a job to do; he was to rule over every living creature and to be fruitful, fill the earth and subdue it. He did not, however, bless man and make him holy, that is, set apart.

In the Ten Commandments, God has decreed that the seventh day be kept holy while man has to obey that instruction as well as all the others. This means that there is something special about the seventh day. In many ways, the seventh day is the ultimate goal of creation. The Lord Jesus, however, clarified this by saying, "The Sabbath was made for man, not man for the Sabbath" (Mark 2: 27 (NIV)). Even though God set the seventh day apart, he did not set it apart to bind people but to set them free.

It is interesting that the idea of a week is apparent in every part of the world. Some countries determine their calendar by the moon while others determine it by the sun. Every group of people needs to know when to plant their crops and when to reap. They need to know when to expect their animals to bear young. Food has to be stored for the times when it doesn't grow but why do we have a seven-day week?

There have been times when people have experimented with a different week. They have tried to have rest on the tenth day rather than the seventh but it doesn't work. People burn out. There is a design imperative in humans to rest on the seventh day.

We know that many people these days work seven days a week and manage to keep going because they want their business to prosper. However, a person who works six days and then has a day's rest actually achieves more in a seven-day period than a person who works over the full seven days. This may not be true if we only consider one or two weeks but it is true in the long term.

Many people suffer burn out in their work lives and they become dry and bitter inside because they don't take the time to rest one day in seven

There is the story of Eric Liddell who was an Olympic runner. It is told in the movie "Chariots of Fire." He was due to run on a Sunday but came from a very strict Christian family. He chose to miss his race and ran another distance in the Paris Olympic Games in 1924. He won the Gold Medal in that event even though it wasn't his favoured event. Some people use this as an example to show that there is a special blessing for people who respect the seventh day as a day of rest.

There are many people whose job forces them to work on the seventh day. Although many Christians claim the blessing of the seventh day has now passed to the first day. The Lord Jesus talked about the priests in the Temple who worked on the seventh day and they did not violate the commandment (See Matthew

13:5). Many priests, pastors and ministers in churches work on the Sunday because that is part of their job.

Some people religiously refuse to work on Sunday. That attitude, however, may become a means of salvation by works if we are not careful. Many Christian students don't study on Sunday and they perform well at their studies. This is more likely to be a general benefit from following the Maker's instructions rather than a specific reward for works done.

Resting one day in seven shows respect for God's wisdom. He is the Creator and knows what is best for his creatures. The question is "Are we willing to trust God and his wisdom and take advantage of his grace of do we want to try and carry the burden ourselves?"

In Mark 6:31 the Lord Jesus told his disciples to go away into a desert place so that they could rest awhile. They had been working so hard and people were coming and going so that they didn't even have time to eat. The Lord didn't want them to burn out so he called them aside to have a break. In this context they were able to eat but they were also able to rest with the Lord and have his grace rest upon them.]

The grace of God rests on us as we take time to be alone with him. We cannot appreciate the beauty of our relationship with him unless we take time to think about him and give thanks for his love.

Relationships

The only way to build a relationship is to spend time with a person. Experts talk about parents spending "quality" time with their children. This is usually a few short minutes where the parent devotes time exclusively to the child. Often the child doesn't want to have the intensity of that quality time. All children want is quantity time, that is, unrestricted access.

Resting for a whole day is giving quantity time to God. That quantity time develops our relationship with God to a much deeper level. We need to do some preparation during the rest of the week so that the tyranny of the urgent doesn't intrude into our time with God. This preparation makes sure that we make our relationship with God a high priority in our lives.

When Israel was in the wilderness they were given manna six days a week. On the sixth day they were told to collect enough for two days. If they tried to keep manna overnight it rotted and was full of worms, those who kept manna from the sixth day found that there was enough for the seventh day as well and it didn't rot. Resting on the seventh day is about the rest of completion. We are completely secure in the embrace of God's love and we have long-term rest if we let God carry the burden

The laws governing the seventh day extended to the seventh year as well. This gives us an extra dimension to our trust in God. It is easier to trust God to supply our needs for one day but what about one year. The seventh day was blessed to such an extent that the blessing extended to the seventh year. After seven periods of seven years the Lord set apart another year, the year of Jubilee, as a further opportunity to sample his grace.

The cycle of creation was complete in six days and the seventh day was blessed in honour of God's creative genius. This was further celebrated by blessing the seventh year. In that year the land was allowed to lie at rest and regenerate. Today, many farmers use fertilisers to force the productivity of their land. They don't allow the land to rest and recuperate.

After many years of using fertilisers the land becomes tired and the crops don't have the same level of nutrients that they had before. The land is longing for its rest but no one gives the land that rest.

Adam was told to fill the earth and subdue it. The earth was given to Adam for a possession so that he could experience a finite tangible expression of God's goodness on a daily basis. Even the earth with all its abundance needed to have to time to rest.

The fiftieth year was another gift of God's grace. Each fifty years all the land reverted to its original owner. Every Israeli had God's inbuilt social security service. Any person who became poor or suffered a set back had the security of the land so that they could be protected.

The Poor and the Weak

God's plan looked forward to a time when there would be poor in the land. When God made Adam and Eve he gave them everything they needed. Even though God is completely innocent when it comes to the question of sin, it did not take him by surprise. God is pure and holy and cannot even bear to tolerate any sin. Never the less, he knew that each person would be a sinner by choice. He knew that sin would bring terrible destruction on the perfect earth that he had made and he prepared to mitigate its effects.

As time went by some people became rich and exploited other people while some became poor and helpless. God set apart the seventh day so that the poor could rest and have some time for themselves and their relationship with God. After slavery was invented some people lost their right to have any freedom at all. God included the guarantee of rest in the Law so that even these poor people could rest and protect themselves from burnout.

Holding Together

Even though God rested from the work of creation on the seventh day, he didn't desert the earth altogether. His rest is a dynamic rest. Colossians 1:17 tells us that the Lord Jesus holds everything together as well. He is God and so he rested on the seventh day when there was nothing left to create. While he rested from the act of creation, he did not rest from the act of sustaining the earth. God's rest is a generous and gracious rest that considers his creature's needs.

God is grace is evident in the fact that he is always in control of the universe. He never rests from his love or his care. His love will continue forever (1 Corinthians 13: 13).

You May Not Eat

Read- Genesis 2: 15-17

God made Adam, a man on the sixth day. This man, Adam, was made to resemble God and it says that God made male and female. This was not an act of creation but God used the resources available on the earth to make the human race. We come from the earth and we return to the earth. No matter is made everything is just recycled by God's grace. He put enough material on the earth to allow the earth to keep going for its entire life without needing any new resources.

Relationship

God made us so that we would resemble him. We know that God is a Spirit but we have bodies. We are not made like God in that we have a body. In fact, the whole of creation is a finite tangible expression of God and his goodness. So, in that sense we resemble God. Sinless humanity is an expression of God's goodness. But there is more to this sentence than just his fact that in many ways trivialises God's grace.

The human race was specifically created in God's own image not just generally. We have an in particular resemblance to God. One of thing about God in this passage is the fact that his name is plural. The word used means that God is three or more. To say this indicates that we worship more than one God is pure blasphemy. This is a plural of majesty. Whenever the name of God is used in this way it always has a singular verb. God, plural, created, singular, and so on. This kind of plural is similar to repetition that is used to indicate superfine quality.

In Numbers 3:9 we can see that God gives the tribe of Levi to Aaron from among all the children of Israel. So God is the supreme and mighty one of superfine quality. But now we have God saying let us make man so that he resembles us. There is more than just simple majesty here. God is complete in every way and did not create the heavens and the earth to improve his own position.

Never the less, God did create us in his own image. One of the reasons that God is complete in every way is that within the Godhead there is perfect unity and agreement of purpose. God has the capacity to form relationships. Man was created with capacity to form relationships.

Not only did God make us so that we could enjoy all his goodness. He made us so that we could have a relationship with him. This does not mean that God needed to have another being outside himself with whom he could have a relationship. God knew that if he made us so that we could have a relationship with him then it would be even better for us.

God adds grace to grace. We have the capacity to enjoy all the good things that God can provide. On top of that we have the capacity to actually form a relationship with God; a relationship of complete dependence and absolute rest.

Purpose

God is always purposeful; he never sleeps or takes a holiday (Psalm 121: 4 and compare 1 Kings 18: 27). He gave this capacity to humanity as well. To be made in God's image includes the dignity of purpose on earth. There are many people today who don't know who they are or where they fit in society and suicide has become an epidemic among both the young and old. If we don't have a reason to be on earth then we feel that there is no reason for us to stay alive.

God delegated his authority to humanity in a local sense. God rules and sustains the Universe and we were told to rule the earth and all its creatures. In exchange for this God provided fruit and grain for his people while the animals had grass and leafy plants. Each day; humanity is to wake to a purpose but on the seventh day we are to wake to rest because we have worked well.

Chapter two tells us that God made Adam first; he used some of the soil of the earth to make man. After the soil was moulded he breathed into his nostrils and gave him life. This is different to all the other animals and plants because they were made alive. God breathed his special purpose into Adam's nostrils and so he commissioned him to the special task of managing this in particular part of God's creation.

In managing the "in particular" part of creation Adam was graciously given and extra dimension of enjoyment of God's goodness and grace. As part of this delegated authority Adam was given the responsibility of naming all the creatures on earth.

Choice

There was one tree in the middle of the garden that Adam was told to keep away from. The fruit of the tree of the knowledge of good and evil was strictly forbidden.

Why would God do all these wonderful things for Adam and then tell him that he couldn't take fruit from one tree. This establishes the principle of choice. God has the capacity to choose. He was not forced to create the world but he freely chose to create. We, who are made to resemble God, have this resemblance as well; we can choose.

God always chooses to do what is good and right. He is never associated with sin in any way and he never chooses to sin. God is consistent; he did not give us the ability to choose so that we might fail. He gave us the ability to choose so that we could choose to enjoy his love. Within our human nature is the ability to enjoy what we choose. In fact, if we choose something and then we get what we choose our enjoyment is increased.

God's plan was that we enjoy his goodness in the richest possible way so he gave us the ability to choose. Here is God's grace, not only can we enjoy God's goodness but we can choose to enjoy God's goodness. God made the earth for our enjoyment and then he increased out capacity to enjoy all the good things that he had made. God has a way of improving everything that he does.

Choice comes with an awesome responsibility. We get what we choose. If we choose to enjoy God's love then we will have the richest possible enjoyment of that love and out enjoyment will increase every day. If we choose not to enjoy God's love then we will get what we choose. With every privilege comes a responsibility.

This applies today. We may make choices and the consequences will come and we cannot really avoid them. Sometimes other people are affected by our choices and sometimes we believe that we are experiencing consequences that we didn't choose. In fact, we are experiencing consequences that we didn't think about when we made our choice.

There is another dimension of grace in consequences as well. When the Lord told the Israelis about their experiences in the desert he said that he had put them into the wilderness for three reasons. (Deuteronomy 8: 2, 16) There were in the wilderness to make them humble, to test them to see if they would obey the Lord and so that it would be good for them in the end.

God allows us to experience hard times because there is sin in the world. He never tests us to see if we will fail. He tests us to make us humble so that we will feel good about God rather than feeling bad about ourselves. We have to learn to trust God without question because that is the only way to really enjoy the full extent of his goodness. If we come through the tests we will be much richer for the experience and our love for God will be deeper and more fulfilling.

We Choose What We Think

The Lord said that anyone could know real peace in their minds if they spent time thinking about him (Isaiah 26:3). We also know that our personality is defined by the way we think (Proverbs 23: 7). The tree in the middle of the garden was given to offer Adam and Eve choice.

The next level is that we can choose what we think. God gave Adam the opportunity to look at the tree every day and think how wonderful it was to have a relationship with God. This is the best relationship that any person can have because it is the only one to which we have to make no contribution other than complete trust.

God's grace reaches out beyond the Garden of Eden to every person on the earth. Each one of us is free to think about our relationship with God and how good it is. No matter what our circumstances we still can choose what we think. Over the years many people have been imprisoned for their faith in God and often they have been tortured as well. Even in these trying circumstances we are able to come to God and pray and enjoy the perfect peace of having a relationship with him.

Out attitude determines the level of enjoyment we have in life. If our attitude is one of gratitude to the Lord for all his grace then we will be able to triumph in any circumstances. On the other hand, the attacks from God's great enemy come into our minds as well. The thought is father to the deed. No one chooses to act against God's grace before they think about acting against God's grace.

People who believe in God can enjoy complete freedom because God has made himself responsible for their future. As long as we spend time thinking about God's grace and thanking him for his love we can have peace of mind.

Wrath

God's wrath should always be considered in relation to choice. When God offered Adam the opportunity to choose he could not become inconsistent himself. If we have the opportunity to choose then God retains his consistency and gives us what we choose. If he were to insulate some people from the consequences of choosing to ignore his love he would then punish those who chose to enjoy his love for doing so.

Many people have a picture of God's wrath as a huge display of all the forces of nature arrayed against a poor defenceless person. If we do something wrong then God will suddenly descend with a huge display of force and destroy the offending person; we just have to hope that God doesn't "get" us today.

"Anger" or "wrath" in the Old Testament usually means a strong emotional outburst of reaction. It is always used of someone who is superior reacting to someone who is inferior. Moses was angry with the Israelis in Exodus 16: 20. He warned them not to keep manna overnight but some of them kept it in their tents and the next morning there was strong smell of decay. These people refused to trust God and obey his commandments.

When a king or ruler becomes angry his anger may be arbitrary or vindictive. When Elijah didn't come out and greet Naaman with the proper protocol he became very angry (see 2 kings 5). His own sense of his personal worth was offended and he left Elijah's home in a fit of rage. After all, he was a great man in Syria and this uncouth, country bumpkin wouldn't even come out and show him respect.

God's anger is never arbitrary or vindictive it is always just and consistent. This kind of anger is a simple step of consequence. God doesn't lose his tempter or throw a tantrum he simply allows people who choose to do without his love to experience the consequences of their choice. God rules the universe and is the source of every good thing. If we want to without God then we do without his goodness as well.

Without God's consistency there is never any real peace. Even though we think that we are peaceful and secure, we can never be completely safe. Someone else can always be offended and we may experience random acts of violence, which destroy our peace and security.

A quick look through history will show how often people have rested secure and lost everything because someone else didn't respect their rights to be secure and at peace. In fact, the concept of the rule of law is really based on God's consistency. He never becomes irrational or unpredictable. God controls the future and he always keeps his promises.

It Is Not Good To Be Alone

Read- Genesis 2: 18, 21-24

The real tapestry of our lives is made up of relationships rather than the things that we own. The richest person in the world would be miserable without any relationships. When God said that it was not good for man to be alone, he indicated that we have been made as social creatures. We made in God's image in a spiritual way so that we could communicate with God and enjoy this communication. We were made in God's image in a physical way as well so that we could enjoy his goodness and be amazed at his majesty and delight in his love.

Relationships

The earth is a finite, tangible expression of all the good things that God has to offer. God is infinite so we cannot know God unless he comes to us. He made the heavens and the earth for us to possess and to show us his greatness in a way that we can understand. Even though made us, we would never be able to know him without him showing himself to us.

Our position is one of complete dependence and we are the recipients of his grace. There is a one-way street of goodness and love coming from God to us. We can respond to his goodness and love by choosing to enjoy the things that he gives or we can choose to reject that love.

God has put men and women together so that they can fulfil special needs in each other in a special way. Men and women can come close to the rest that God wants for us when we are complete in a relationship. God defined that one man should be with one woman and they would not be alone. If there is more than one man or more than one woman then rest will never truly be available.

Ecclesiastes 4: 9-11 explains why this is so. When two people are together they can help each other. If one falls over then the other is there to help them. Even today experts advise that people travelling in remote places go with other people so that when one is in trouble the other can help. One person will get cold when the weather is cold but two people can huddle together and keep each other warm.

Rope makers know that when strands of cord are put together they strengthen each other. A rope made of three cords is much stronger than three cords used together. This means that any relationship between a man and a woman is much stronger when they include God. The ultimate relationship is marriage and that is made strong when God is included. The real enjoyment of this gift of God's grace comes when the marriage partners both submit to God's order.

While it is good for families to help each other the relationship between man and woman will never be complete until the go out by themselves and live together. A relationship between a man and a woman can be complete without children but children come when God's command to be fruitful is obeyed. Of course, sometimes God, in his wisdom withholds children.

From The Side

The Lord made Adam fall asleep and then he took a rib from Adam's side. Many commentators interpret this fact in the following way. If God had taken a bone from Adam's head his partner would have been chosen to rule over him. If a foot bone was taken then the partner would be there to serve Adam but the bone was taken from Adam's side so she could go with him and share in his work.

In some societies women are brought up to serve men while in other societies women try to rule their men and make all the decisions. Both of these are wrong according to God's plan. Adam and Eve were made to be together and to do God's work on the earth.

One of the major benefits of having a man and woman together is procreation. A man cannot produce babies with another man and a woman cannot produce babies with another woman. One man and one woman necessary and sufficient for procreation. It is possible for friendship to exist between men and men and between men and women but there will never be full satisfaction. One man was created to be with one woman and they are told to leave their parents and to be together.

Procreation requires an equal input from the man and the woman. Some cultures believe that the woman is a garden where the man plants the seed. This makes the woman inferior in the process. If the woman is just a garden then a man can have more than one wife.

Without Conflict

God, however, in grace chose to give order in this relationship. Adam was created first and God put him in charge of the garden. His job was to cultivate and keep the garden. God asked Adam to name all the animals so that he would be familiar with them as he cared for them.

Eve was put in the garden to help Adam. God, in grace, set up this order so that true rest could be available in the marriage relationship. When there is no agreement there is always strife. Any marriage that is a power struggle wears both partners out and they will never enjoy the benefits of not being alone.

Proverbs 21: 9, 19; 25: 4; 27:15 all talk about a contentious woman. The root idea behind the word "contentious" is “rule”. If the helper tries to rule then there is strife. All the benefits of being together are lost.

Men and women can only enjoy the fruits of having a “soul mate” when they share a common goal. If people do not work towards a common goal they don’t have anything to share.

The proper order in marriage is: God is the head of the relationship, he gives the man a task to do and the woman is to help him with this task. As long as the woman is willing to work with her husband then there will be peace. As long as the man treats his wife like an equal and includes her in his decisions she will feel secure.

God rested on the seventh day because he finished his work. He plans that each one of us should know the rest of completion, that is, security. In his grace he has made this security available in human relationships but they only work when his order is followed.

There is a belief today that men and women are different because they come from different planets but this is wrong. Men and women come from the same planet but God made them with different roles. God in grace chose to offer peace, security and significance to every man and woman as long as they choose to enjoy his goodness and accept his wisdom.

Increased Grace

Read Genesis 3- 1-13

Romans 5: 20 (Good News Bible) tells us, "Where sin increased, God's grace increased much more." In Genesis 1 and 2 there is a river of grace flowing wide and deep now that sin enters the world that river changes into a mighty flood.

More Grace

But how is it possible for God's grace to increase? The Lord himself, said, "I, the Lord, do not change" (Malachi 3:6, NASB 95). If the Lord doesn't change then surely his grace cannot increase.

God's grace can be compared to a mother's love. When the mother has her first child there is enough love for that child. However, after some time the mother will have more children and her love will be large enough to include all of her children. Her potential to love is much greater than the love she gives away at any time. The same is true of God. His potential for grace covers the sins of more than 6.3 billion people but, before there was sin, his grace was large enough to encompass the Universe and every living creature within.

Before sin, the river of God's grace was running throughout the earth. At this stage his grace was making sure that his creatures enjoyed the best of his abundance. They were still in a rich and satisfying relationship with God. He would come and spend time with them every day. All Adam and Eve had to do was see the tree and know that God loved them. Every morning they could chose to accept God's generosity and live in paradise. Every evening they could rest secure in the knowledge that God was in control and they lacked nothing.

By themselves, Adam and Eve could ask for nothing more. They were basking in the fullness of God's rest. When God was finished, there was nothing left to do. At the same time, there was nothing for more for Adam and Eve to possess.

The Snake

It would seem that the writer is talking about a particular snake when he says, "Now the snake was the most cunning animal that the Lord God had made." This is more than just any snake. There is a spiritual evil here as well as a material evil.

At this stage, there was no sin in the universe. Some people say that Satan sinned before the Lord created the world. Other people put forward the theory that Satan sinned during the Gap of Genesis 1:2. If either of these were the case why did God look at the world he had made and see that everything was very good?

The snake is Satan, God's great enemy. There is no evidence to suggest that Satan had sinned before this but this act is a great act of rebellion. He tried to lure Adam and Eve away from God's love and trust his twisted scheme. Perhaps Satan sins for the first time here as well. There is no doubt that he had spent some time thinking about what he is going to do and devising his plan.

In both Isaiah 42: 8 and 48: 11 the Lord states that he will not share his glory with anyone else. This means that the Lord is the best and every other creature takes a lower place. Satan was the greatest of all the angels. There are three archangels talked about, Michael, Gabriel and Lucifer. Lucifer was the greatest of these but he wasn't content to be under God. He wanted the glory for himself. He also has an intense hatred of man. He was jealous of the relationship between God and man. Man was created in God's image but not Satan. Satan worked to destroy the relationship between God and the human race.

Satan knew the truth but he is the father of lies (John 8: 44). He uses lies to deceive and lead people astray. He tried to deceive God as well but this didn't work. (The book of Job tells the story of how Satan tried to deceive God and Satan's hatred for Job. In the end Job has a much richer and sweeter relationship with God so the whole exercise was a failure as far as Satan is concerned.)

The Fall

Satan began his deception by asking Eve a question. "Is it true that God has said?" He wants to put doubt in Eve's mind so that she no longer trusted the Lord completely. "Did he really say that?" Eve told the truth in answer to this question saying that they weren't allowed to eat the fruit from one particular tree.

Satan continued the deception by telling her that they wouldn't actually die. Eve had already listened to the snake and was now thinking about what he had said. She should have realised that something was wrong the moment she heard the snake talking because animals don't talk. Adam was nearby too but he made no effort to stop the conversation.

The thought is father to the deed (See Matthew 15: 18). Whenever we think about something then we are in danger of action. Eve doubted God and his pure grace. She looked at the fruit and it looked nice to eat. Not only did the fruit look nice to eat it would also make a person wise. After some thought, Eve took the fruit and ate it.

Adam was standing right there as well because Eve immediately gave Adam some fruit to eat as well. When Eve took the lead, she was no longer helping Adam: she was setting his goals for him. Perhaps this is why Satan chose to tempt Eve; she was not completely satisfied to trust Adam to take the lead in everything.

Satan was not happy that Adam and Eve were made in God's image and they had the personal relationship with God. He wanted to destroy that because he believed that he deserved the prominent place in the Universe. Eve wanted to take a more significant role in the affairs of the garden so Satan attacked her. Adam was not innocent either. He made no effort to exercise his leadership.

There is evidence of God's grace in the fact that both Adam and Eve sinned. If one had sinned and not the other they would both have been alone. At least in their spiritual death they were able to have a companion. This is not to say that God was responsible in any way for the sin of either Adam or Eve. Both of them chose to sin without any Divine input.

They Were Naked

As soon as they ate the fruit Adam and Eve knew that they were naked. There was no time lag between eating and understanding. God made them a promise and it was immediately fulfilled. They were spiritually dead from that moment and they realised that nothing was hidden before God. They had not excuses and no way of deceiving God.

They tried to do something about their situation by making clothes out of fig leaves. Fig leaves are quite large and provide some measure of protection from the realisation that they are naked.

There is delayed judgement as well as immediate judgement here. The moment they sinned Adam and Eve began to die. They lost their innocence and knew the difference between good and evil. From that moment there has always been a struggle between good and evil in every human heart. They were afraid of God now even though they had known no fear before.

Where Are You?

Now God had come, as usual to walk with Adam and Eve at the time of the gentle breeze. This is probably the evening when the breeze comes and cools us from the heat of the day. God knew what had happened. He misses nothing on the earth. He knows where every sub atomic particle is at every moment of time. Yet he called out to Adam and Eve to ask them where they were.

Adam made his admission. Fear had come between the sinners and their holy God. Adam knew that he has sinned and is afraid of meeting God. He was ashamed of his actions and knew that he has betrayed the best friend that he would ever have. God had given Adam so much but Adam didn't appreciate it and tried to take the one thing that God kept back.

God gave Adam and Eve an opportunity to own the fact that they had sinned. He was not in any way surprised by their sin or concerned about their whereabouts. Almighty God is everywhere in the Universe and nothing escapes his all seeing eyes yet he gave Adam the chance to own the fact that he had sinned. Forgiveness is a gift that belongs to the injured party. A person may beg for forgiveness but they can never demand it as a right. God is ready to forgive but he will not forgive unless the sinner owns their sin.

Adam began his sinful life by hiding from God and then he blamed Eve for the sin that he freely chose to commit. God gave

Adam the opportunity to repent but Adam chose to blame someone else. Next, God asks Eve and she blamed the snake.

Adam actually blamed God when he tried to explain away his sin. He told God that it was the woman that God gave him who caused all the problems. Both Adam and Eve wanted to be like God. They wanted to have God's glory for themselves but there is only room for one God in the Universe.

God is the best and he must always be treated with the respect that he deserves. As soon as someone wants to be in control of their lives they try to be the best and attempt to take God's glory away from him. There is only enough room in the Universe for one person who is the best. Anyone who takes that away from God cannot be in a relationship with God.

God is the best and anyone who has a relationship with God has to acknowledge that fact. But God is gracious and is willing to forgive if we admit that we have tried to take his glory from him. When Adam and Eve sinned, God proved himself to be gracious by giving them an opportunity to own their sin.

Grace In The Curse

Read- Genesis 3: 13-19

It seems as though Satan might have been right when he told Eve that she would not surely die. As soon as they ate the fruit they were afraid of God and rightly so. But they began to die immediately; the slow, painful process of physical death started to work its way through their bodies and they immediately they died emotionally and spiritually. From that very moment their relationship with God was broken and they could nothing to reverse the process. They also began to have trouble in their human relationships as the selfish desires of sin took over from the servant desires that God placed in their hearts. Can anyone be more dead than that? Surely not!

You Shall Die

We live in a day when researchers tell us regularly that they have discovered that something we eat or do will make us die. The statistical truth is that everyone who breathes, eats or sleeps is going to die. 100% of people who died in the past did these things. Of course, not breathing, not eating and not sleeping will also cause us to die more quickly. However, breathing, eating and sleeping are not immediate causes of death.

Before Adam and Eve ate from the fruit of the tree they were not dying, as soon as they ate the fruit from the tree they began to die. God's justice usually takes time because God is gracious. He delays his justice to give sinners a chance to own the fact that they have sinned. There is always room for reconciliation when we admit that we have sinned. Adam and Eve had a chance to repent when God called out to them and then he gave them more time to repent.

In 2 Chronicles 30: 18 we have a situation where Israel had not obeyed the commandments and some of them had taken the Passover without being properly clean. Hezekiah, the king, prayed for the people and asked the good Lord to pardon every one of them. This was another case where God, the injured party, was able to offer the gift of forgiveness and pardon the sinner. He gave his sinning creatures time to repent and time to ask him for forgiveness.

God's grace delays punishment so that the sinner has time to repent.

The Serpent

The serpent was different to Adam and Eve. He deliberately set out to deceive. Satan knew that he was doing the wrong thing but his hatred of man and jealousy of God drove him on; all he wanted to do was destroy.

God gave us the ability to choose as an act of grace. We are allowed to choose so that when we choose to enjoy God's love our enjoyment will be much richer. Day by day we see the wonderful things that God has made on the earth. Every day we are reminded of God's goodness as we see the finite, tangible expressions of goodness. Our experiences are given to us to improve our enjoyment of God's love, majesty and grace. We can choose to enjoy them and have all the good things that God designed us to enjoy or we can choose to do without God and get what we ourselves can provide. We can accept goodness from God, who controls the future, or we can get what our finite, tangible capacity can provide.

Each person can have a life that is tyrannised by the arbitrary or they can be part of God's perfect plan that works for the good of his people. Never the less, God has a special punishment for those who lead others astray or continually reject him. Proverbs 6: 13-15 speaks about the person who leads others astray and it says that such a person will be broken without remedy. Proverbs 29: 1 speaks about a person who is corrected many times but becomes more stubborn. That man will suddenly be broken beyond remedy. When God talks about Moses asking

Pharaoh to release Israel from slavery we see that, at first, Pharaoh hardens his heart but later God hardens Pharaoh's heart.

Satan came to attack Adam and Eve with evil in his heart. This enemy was not working for their good or for God's glory and God condemned him to his own choice. There is no remedy for the serpent; he can look forward to conflict forever. The children of Adam and Eve would be at war with the descendants of the serpent forever.

Not only is there a physical battle but there is a spiritual battle as well. One day, the great spiritual descendant of Eve will come and defeat the serpent completely. With the entrance of sin comes the promise of Satan's defeat. One day a person will come who can restore the perfect relationship between God and man.

Fruitful and Multiply

Whenever we have a relationship with God it is always on the basis of his greatness and our weakness in comparison. We were created to be completely dependent on God and to receive good things from him throughout our lives. In order to improve our appreciation of his love, God gave us the capacity to choose. But God is always consistent. When we make a choice he will always give us the consequences of our choice, even though, at times, he delays the consequences in grace.

Remarkably, God uses the consequences of our actions to work for good in our lives (see Deuteronomy 5: 23; 6: 24). One of the most important aspects of God's application of consequences is to restore us to the original state where we realised that we needed him for everything. God is the best, all the glory belongs to him and as long as we accept that fact and adapt to it we will have peace with God.

Adam and Eve sinned and God applied consequences to their choice but God applied them in such a way as to restore their former status before God. Of course, they can no longer enjoy the relationship as it was before, they have sinned and are spiritually dead. Never the less, God was working towards restoration.

Before the fall, Adam and Eve were part of the command to be fruitful and multiply. The only way they could obey this command was by reproduction. As the animal numbers increased by the same method, Adam and Eve would need to have children so that their offspring could care for the garden and the animals as God had told them.

Not only was Eve given the responsibility of helping Adam in his work, she was given the physical capacity to bear children as well. While Adam was in charge of caring for the present, Eve was in charge of the future. She bore the children and she nurtured them.

God punished Eve by affecting her capacity to reproduce. The entire process is now accompanied by pain. This is not, however, just an example of God being vindictive and arbitrary. Eve is given the chance to choose to be humble before God on a regular basis and be reminded of his greatness and love.

God's grace continued in the future relationship between Adam and Eve. As part of her curse, Eve was put in a relationship where she has to submit to Adam. Before that she had to submit to God and share with her husband, now she is cursed to submit to her husband. In this submission, however, Eve would find peace.

She would be able to live with her husband and he would love her, as she was willing to accept his leadership. Once again, God's grace shone out to Eve, she could have the God's rest in her home and she could have the God's peace in her life as long as she was willing to accept that God is God.

Not only did God give Eve the chance for peace in her home, he gave her the important task of controlling the future. She would bear the children and nurture them so she would be first important influence in their lives. She would be able to mould the future of the human race because a child tends to keep to those things that they have learnt while they are very young (Proverbs 22: 6).

Eve was given the promise that, one day, a spiritual offspring of hers would come and defeat Satan. This offspring is said to be her seed. Even though sin marred the relationship God was, in grace, giving them opportunities to submit to him again and know his peace.

Significance

Of all God's creatures, Adam was the only one given a special responsibility. He became God's representative and agent on God's earth. He was put in charge of the garden and all the creatures and was given free reign, under God, to exercise his responsibility. Every day God would come and spend time with Adam and Eve and they would enjoy his goodness and grace. Adam knew that God loved and respected him because God gave him and important task. There is not much advantage in being made in God's image if we don't have extra privileges.

Now that Adam had sinned and he was no longer worthy to be God's representative on the earth. God would not have a sinner as his agent because God would then be associated with sin but he is pure and perfect in every way; Adam should no longer have a role to play. While Eve had control of the future, God, in his grace, gave Adam control over the present. What should have been a pleasure to him now becomes a chore. He had to work hard to produce his food instead of receiving it freely from God's hand.

Adam was still given an important role to fulfil. He was responsible for feeding and caring for his family. Every day as he went out to earn his bread he is would be reminded as he suffered that God is God. This task was given to make Adam feel as though he still had a role to play on the earth and to remind him of God's greatness.

God was gracious with Adam as well. He could daily choose to submit to God and accept that God is the best. In his daily work, Adam could see God's handiwork in the world, which is the finite tangible expression of God's goodness. As he worked he could learn to accept that God is the best and give him the glory. Any man can now choose to have peace with God as he accepts that God knows best and give God the glory.

Substitution

Adam and Eve tried to clothe themselves in leaves. Now leaves don't make good clothes because they take only a few days to dry out and crumble. These clothes would not have offered any lasting protection. When the sun was hot they offered no protection and they wouldn't keep the cold out. The first people knew that they were naked and they were ashamed but God came in grace. He provided animal skins for them so that they could have clothes that would keep them warm when things were cold and shelter them from the sun when it was hot.

No doubt, Adam and Eve would have persisted with the leaves and been constantly ashamed as the leaves broke and failed to give the protection. But, in spite of their sin, God showed them how to find decent clothes.

In order for animal skins to be made available, animals had to be sacrificed. God established a new principal that covers all his dealings with sinful humanity. Adam and Eve were given time to repent of their sin and confess to God that they were sinners but blood was shed for their sin. God in his grace established the wonderful principal of substitution. When a person sins they can shed the blood of another creature which will cover their sin. This process had to continue as long as people sinned. Every time we sin there has to be a sacrifice made so that a substitute can die for our sins. This is the flood of grace.

The special promise made to Eve foreshadowed another Substitute who would, one day become a permanent sacrifice so that animals will no longer have to be sacrificed as temporary substitutes. God promised that, in the future, there would be a substitute who would be able to bruise Satan's head. Satan would suffer a permanent defeat and there would no longer be any need for sacrifices.

Live Forever

Some people today are talking about being able to live for one hundred and fifty or two hundred years or even more. Throughout history there has been a great interest in eternal life. One good example is the Pharaohs of Egypt building pyramids and mummifying their bodies so that they could have some of their current status in the after life.

God, however, as part of the curse, put angels beside the tree of life so that Adam and Eve would not eat from that tree and live forever. There is grace in this as well. Even though we may want to live forever our bodies are affected by sin and they begin to decay while we live. While it is true that some people live past one hundred years without suffering too much, most people become less mobile and experience more pain, as they grow older.

Imagine being confined to bed, in pain and incontinent for thousands of years. There is no joy in this. God has allowed death to intervene so that people can escape the pain of their decaying bodies. There is a chance to experience relief and that is a gift of God's grace. People who admit that they are sinners and repent can be reconciled to God by his grace. These people can restore their relationship with God because God himself has redeemed them and they can escape from the endless cycle of pain and decay.

Noah

Read- Genesis 6

One of the sad facts of sin is that we experience its consequences in our lives. The law of action and consequence, that God gave in grace to improve our enjoyment of his goodness, works its inevitable conclusion.

Evil Multiplies

As soon as Adam and Eve decided that they would try and take God's glory for themselves they entered a new phase of their existence. The progress from the pure worship of God to the base worship of the creature is inevitable. As soon as people begin to ignore God they fall away into all kinds of debauchery. However,

God's grace still shone out as he kept a pure line. The promise came to Eve that one of her descendants would eventually conquer the serpent. God maintained the perfect line through whom this perfect person would come. Adam and Eve had a good son called Seth but Cain was abandoned to his evil ways after he killed his brother Abel.

The descendants of the good line and the bad line populated the world, side by side. Both of the sons brought offerings to the Lord. Cain tried to show God his own glory but Abel came in humility giving all the glory to God. Even though there was sin in the world, God in grace kept some people who gave the glory to God. It would be impossible, later, for the perfect descendant to come from a polluted line.

Satan entered into Cain's heart, even though he still had the choice to defeat this evil desire, and he killed his brother because God accepts those who bring him glory and rejects those who take the glory for themselves. God still gives a person the choice to give him the glory even though they may be living a life filled with sin. Eventually people become confirmed in their choice. At first we can choose to sin or not to sin but later, as we harden ourselves in our sin, God will harden our hearts in the way that we have chosen. This is the message of Proverbs 29: 1.

This is the godly line that God preserved so that the promised deliverer would still come. Adam, Seth, Enosh, Kenan, Mahahalel, Jared, Enoch, Methuselah, Lamech and Noah.

In Genesis 6 we see that the human race had become fruitful and they started to fill the earth. At this stage the good line began to mix with the bad line and the whole population was in danger of being polluted. In order to prevent this God chose to destroy the earth with the flood. This was still an act of grace. Were the whole population to be polluted then we would all be condemned to permanent spiritual death and complete and irretrievable separation from God.

With the coming of sin and its ugly consequences another part of the character of God joined the river of grace. Grace is a gift that is given to people who don't deserve the gift but mercy occurs when we don't get what we deserve. Every person on the earth deserved to experience eternal separation from God but God, in mercy, kept the possibility of a renewed relationship open.

Separation

Throughout the history of Israel the Lord insisted on separation. This insistence was a consequence of the problems experienced during these days. The biggest enemy of intolerance is sexual attraction. From stories like Shakespeare's *Romeo and Juliet* to many real modern day romances people who are meant to remain separate have fallen in love and defied the bans set by their communities.

In the former Republic of South Africa there was a crime called miscegenation. This was put on the statute books because there was sexual contact between the races.

In Numbers 25 we read how the Israeli men were filled with desire for the Midianite women and they risked God's anger. Phinehas the priest took a spear and killed a couple who were unashamed about disobeying the Law and the plague stopped.

King Solomon was involved with many foreign women. He wasn't some kind of sex maniac but married women from other nations to make alliances. In those days, a king would give his daughter to another king and she would be held in the palace as a ransom so that there wouldn't be war between the nations. Solomon chose to rely on these alliances rather than trust in God to defend his borders. These women led Solomon astray and the king who began so well finished his life worshipping foreign gods with his foreign women.

The sad thing about the modern trend to call remaining separate a bad thing is that everybody tends to move towards the lowest common denominator. There are cases where godly people can work with others and, by the power of the Holy Spirit, lead them to submit to God's ways but this only happens when the godly person remains separate in their mind.

God, in his grace, knows the human heart and he has called on us to devote our hearts to his ways and to love him. An abbreviated form of the commandment states: "You shall love the LORD your God with all your heart and with all your soul and with all your might" (Deuteronomy 6:5). This wholehearted devotion is not possible without separation from things that will pollute our minds.

Where there was no separation the whole world would become polluted and God would then have to destroy everyone as he came close to doing during the days of Noah.

The Ark

God told Noah to build and ark that would able to carry Noah, his family and the animals of the earth through the coming flood. At this stage there had never been any rain on the earth for a mist came up and watered all the plants (Genesis 2:6).

Noah was a man of great faith. He obeyed the Lord even though he had never seen rain and didn't understand what God meant. This man was part of the godly line and he hadn't polluted himself in any way. The Lord God was pleased with Noah and he found favour before God.

Noah began to build his ark. This was an act of grace on God's part. Most of the population of the earth was polluted by sin and God could no longer bear to have such sin on the earth that he had made. Never the less, God promised that a spiritual descendant of Eve would, one day, defeat the serpent and restore the relationship between God and man to its former intimacy. God was gracious in that he maintained the godly line by preserving one of its members.

In Genesis 6: 3 God put a limit on the time for sinners. He promised that their time would run in out one hundred and twenty years.

For one hundred and twenty years, Noah built the ark in the exact proportions that God had given to him. During all these years, everyone could see or hear about Noah's act. God took his time to deliver this punishment so that the people on the earth could take time and repent. All sinners have to do is take responsibility for their sin and then there is a basis for reconciliation and forgiveness.

God's grace is best seen in this dimension of his character. He is quick to bless and quick to reward but he takes his time to judge. He waits for long time so that people can have a chance to repent of their sin and seek to restore the relationship that they were created to enjoy.]

God, however, in grace, will never sacrifice those who choose his love for the sake of those who choose to ignore him. The rule always stays the same: "You get what you choose." Noah chose to obey God and God saved him from the flood. The others chose to ignore God and they all perished in the flood.

Delays

Even though we have seen how God is quick to bless, there are times when God tests his own people. Noah had to wait for one hundred and twenty years as well. During all that time he had to rely on God's command and promise. There was no real evidence in nature or from other people that this would happen.

God often gives his people testing times and these may last for many years. This is evidence of God's grace. As we wait and trust the Lord our relationship with him becomes sweeter and richer. When there are no distractions and we have to trust in the Lord and have nothing else then we can focus on him entirely.

Day after day Noah had to go back to the Lord in prayer and seek comfort and assurance because there was no one else to look to. His family helped him build the ark but they were obeying their father. Noah had the vision from the Lord and he drew closer to the Lord each day as he worked on the task.

After the flood was over and things began to improve Noah was not so dependant on God. He made wine and got drunk. This would never have happened during the days when he was building the ark.

Even in the hardest times, the river of grace flows wide and fast.

The Rainbow

Read- Genesis 8 and 9

In Genesis 1: 9, we have the Lord gathering all the water together in one place and distinguishing it from the land. It would seem that there was one large expanse of water and one expanse of land. There was no rain in those days and only four rivers, the Pishon, the Gihon, the Tigris and the Euphrates.

It is interesting that countries in the New World often name towns, rivers and other places of interest after similar features in their home country. When the people came out of the ark they chose to name two of the rivers in their new country after two of the rivers that were in the place they lived before the flood. This didn't mean that these rivers survived some kind of local flood.

One Place

When we get to Genesis 8 we see that the flood began when the fountains of the great deep and the floodgates of the sky were opened. These fountains had previously fed the rivers. After the flood we discover that the Tigris and the Euphrates are two rivers, in the Fertile Crescent, but the others are no longer near them. The name Pishon no longer appears in the Bible. Gihon is the name of a place and is mentioned in 1 Kings 1: 45 where it is the name of a sacred spring. This name appears in four other places (1 Kings 1:33, 38, 45; 2 Chronicles 32: 30; 33: 14) where it is a place name associated with Jerusalem and probably the same spring. Gihon in Genesis 2 is said to flow through the land or Cush, there is some argument about the exact location of Cush in this context.

In 1912 a German astronomer and meteorologist called Alfred L Wegener, proposed a theory that all the world's continents had been joined into one super continent[xx]. Later this continent broke up and the continents drifted away to form the current continents. There is a considerable amount of fossil and geological evidence to support this theory. The first continent was called Pangaea, which split into two continents, Laurasia and Gondwanaland. Later the continents drifted and further divided to form the continents, as we know them today. Patrick Blackett, a Nobel Prize winner, showed that Palaeomagnetism supports this theory[xxi].

In time the Continental Drift theory became know as Plate Tectonics. In this theory the world is seen as having a number of fairly thin, rigid plates. These plates are in constant motion. As the Plates move the large fault lines between the converging and diverging plates are unstable. Around the Pacific Rim we have a region known as the "Ring of Fire" caused by this movement.

When the flood began, the fountains of the great deep were opened. Suddenly the stability of the great continent was lost and as it broke up the water gushed up from deep storehouses. Water poured down from heaven and water flooded up from below. Once the landmass was cut loose it became unstable and began to move around. God, in his grace, has shown us the truth many millennia before man first began to consider the idea.

The Fountains of the Deep

The fountains of the great deep and the floodgates of the sky were opened. This means that during the course of the flood, water came down from heaven, that is, there was rain. Before this there had never been rain on the earth. A mist watered the earth. As well as the rain, water came up from beneath the earth. Somewhere underneath the land there was a large store of underground water. Perhaps this water was the source of the mist that came up.

In many parts of the world, rivers are fed by rain and by melting snows but there are also rivers that begin with springs. These springs come from the water table. There are also artesian basins in other parts of the earth and water comes up from the earth, under pressure, for plants and animals to use. This is another act of grace on God's part. He provides water when water is needed even though it may not come from rivers or rain. He freed up the fountains of the deep even though sin was so bad on the earth that he had to destroy the majority of humanity.

The Flood

The rain lasted for forty days and nights. Sometimes, in the Old Testament, the term forty days, or forty years, means "a long time" but there is no reason to suppose that this was longer than forty solar days. While the flood began with the fountains of the deep being opened, it kept raining for forty days.

The Lord brought this about because sin had become so bad on the earth. If this situation had been allowed to flourish then earth would have become the same as hell. Even today, there are some regimes on earth where things have become so sinful that it is like living in hell on earth. While it may be good for those who are in power, most of the population suffers extreme hardship. This is the reason that there are so many refugees scattered around the world today. Many people scoff and talk about economic refugees but there are also genuine refugees who fear for their lives every day.

God, in his grace saw that sin was rampant and he felt sorry for the people of the earth. At this stage they were all close together on the one large continent and there was only one language. All the people suffered under the same fearful rule. It is said that we get the governments that we deserve and this was true in those days as well. Apart from the godly line, the people had set themselves up as God and every form of depravity flourished. It is impossible to draw back from this kind of wantonness once it has taken hold in your life. It is only God's grace and power that can deliver a life from complete depravity.

All of the people alive on the earth in those days were victims of their own choice. They all followed the way Cain's example and tried to take the glory that belonged to God for themselves. The earth itself was suffering under the cruel rule of mankind who had ignored God and followed their own evil ways.

After the forty days of rain, water remained over the earth for another one hundred and fifty days. After the deluge the mud slowly settled back down and the water receded until the ark was able to rest on the top of the mountains of Ararat.

Security

After the Flood, God made Noah a promise. He said that he would never curse the earth again because of man's sin neither would he destroy every living thing. That is, apart from the people and animals that were saved in the ark. God also swore that he would make sure that there was seedtime and harvest, cold and heat, summer and winter, day and night as long at the earth continued.

One important feature of our age is the proclamation of rights. The United States was founded on a Constitution that restricted the power of the three levels of government to persecute the people. They had all come from places where there was persecution and minorities had no rights. In order to ensure that their own people were spared from the whim of a despot they built a new system full of safeguards. Soon after the Constitution was proclaimed they amended it to include a Bill of Rights. This guaranteed individual freedom.

In our world there is no child born who has the right to its mother's love and no person alive has the right to claim the next moment. Where did this idea of individual rights come from? God in his grace gave us certain guarantees. We know that the cycle of summer and winter will continue and that day will follow night as long this earth continues to exist. We all need to have some sense of security. Whenever it rains and we see the rainbow we know that God has promised us that the cycle of day and night, springtime and harvest, summer and winter will continue.

Our western society is based on the concept of the rule of law. We want to know that we can always expect the same outcome in the same circumstances. In the days when Nebuchadnezzar ruled in Babylon, he was not bound by any law (See Daniel 5:19). You could be innocent under the law today but if you did the same thing tomorrow you may be put to death. Imagine if we had to live our lives without any sense of continuity at all.

God has placed a constitution on the earth and promised that he will abide by the rules that he has set. This is a supreme act of grace on his part.

Tree Rings And Sedimentary Strata

The cycle of summer and winter is evident in most deciduous trees. It is possible to tell how old a tree is by boring a hole into the middle and taking a core sample. Every year there are rings: a dark ring of slow growth for the winter and a light ring of faster growth for the summer. In the winter there is less sunlight and the plant produces less food so it goes into a slow growth phase to protect itself.

All around the world there are layers of sedimentary rocks. We are told that these strata took many years to form yet they are uniform throughout each level. How could the strata be uniform while the tree rings change for each year?

When the earth spent one hundred and fifty days under the water of the flood it continued to rotate and move around the sun. At the same time the moon moved around the earth. Wherever the moon moved it pulled some of the water towards it and there were gigantic tides.

While the tides ebbed and flowed in the huge the mass of water, the mud and silt that was stirred up the by the fountains of the deep and the rain began to settle. The water moved forward and backward and the suspended solids settled. At some stage the settling solids became so dense that they no longer were able to move and there was a sheer line. During the next tide the same things happened. This is why we have uniform layers in the sedimentary rocks. They were formed in less than twelve hours.

Every time we see the strata in a cutting at the side of the road, we can appreciate the grace of God. Even though the people on the earth were being punished for their extreme sin, God kept the cycles of the earth going so that there would be consistency. We know from this that we can trust God absolutely. He will never change and he will never dam the river of his abundant grace.

Renewal

Not only did the Lord make a sure promise of security to Noah and all his descendants. He renews the implied promise in creation. The Lord made the earth, in particular, for Adam and his descendants to possess. When Noah came out of the ark, God told him to fill the earth with people and that he gave all the animals of the earth to Noah and his descendants. The only thing that they are not allowed to eat is the blood of animals. This looks forward to a future day when the blood of animals will be shed for the forgiveness of sin.

God punished all the earth because sin had become so bad that every person and animal alive was under severe penalty. Now that sin has been dealt with in the most severe way, God's grace shines out brightly. Everything that was formerly given is promised again and almost without condition. People have to be careful with blood. Because man has been made in God's image, his blood is sacred.

No person should be allowed to take another's life without suffering the extreme penalty. Later, in the law this is mitigated, to exclude circumstances where someone takes another's life without malice or plan.

We live in a day when people talk about rehabilitation of killers and argue that the death penalty is not a deterrent for further murder so we have to abolish it. The death penalty is only about justice. It is abhorrent to think that we would take one person's life so that we can influence another's behaviour. The death penalty was never intended as a deterrent. God believes life is sacred so he demands that one life is forfeit when that person takes another's life. As for rehabilitation, God demands justice. Action requires consequence and we cannot expect to insulate one person from the consequences of their actions so that they can become a better member of society. Rehabilitation should only come after the demands of justice have been met. If we place the creature above the creator we try to take God's glory and apply it to ourselves. As we are sinful the consequences of this will be a totally debauched world where no person is safe or secure.

Even this is a demonstration of God's grace. He wants us to enjoy his goodness without the perversion sin robbing us of any sense of security.

Babel

Read- Genesis 11

The Lord told Noah and his family to be fruitful and multiply in the earth. They were obedient and followed the Lord's commandment. There is grace here as well, God has made provision for his people and the earth is sufficiently bountiful to provide for all of God's creation.

Be Fruitful

God created the heavens and the earth so that we could enjoy the benefits of his goodness. Even though sin entered the world and our enjoyment of this goodness was greatly restricted; God still made it possible for his people to own the earth and enjoy the benefits that the earth could provide. Sin may have restricted our access to a complete relationship with God but God has not changed. He encouraged his people to spread out and fill the earth and to enjoy all the good things that are available.

At this stage the land was rich and prosperous but required hard work; this was part of the curse.

The Same Language

At this stage everyone spoke the same language so they preferred to stay close to each other rather than spread out and fill the whole earth as the Lord had told them to do. What is the use of having a large and fertile earth if everyone stays close together?

At this time there were still wild animals living in close proximity to people so the gathered together and formed communities for protection. In order to protect themselves from the animals the people built walls to secure their families, their homes and their domestic animals.

The temptation that Satan used to seduce Adam and Eve away from God's care was still being used. Even today we still want to be like God and be in control of our circumstances. The people of that day wanted to have eternal life. Before Adam and Eve sinned they had eternal life but when they sinned they experienced death, three kinds of death. They were immediately dead in the spiritual sense because they had no relationship with God. They were emotionally dead because they were unable to form complete human relationships without the foundation of a relationship with God and they began the long, painful, slow process of physical death.

Sin tells us that having eternal life will satisfy our need to be worthwhile in the world. We want to make a name for ourselves. After all, a person's life is like the morning mist[xxii], after we die there isn't much left behind. By the time a person's grandchildren are dead there is virtually nothing left to remember them by.

King Solomon tells us that it is better to be a live dog than a dead lion[xxiii]. When a person is dead none of their relationships is of any value to them. However we want things to be otherwise so we each seek to make an eternal name for ourselves.

Before the people on earth built the tower of Babel they wanted to earn some kind of satisfaction in their desire for eternal life and they wanted to be like God so that they could have a great reputation for themselves.

As soon as people try to take control of the situation we lose contact with God and his greatness and then the earth becomes darkened[xxiv]. The earth becomes debased by sin and God would need to step in and destroy the earth again. However, God promised that this would never happen again.

Babble

As God's creatures we must understand that we are weak and totally dependant on God[xxv]. Without God we can do nothing and we are nothing. When we seek to take over God's place on the earth then we are in danger of complete separation from God. As long as we are alive there is an opportunity for God's grace to work in our lives so that the relationship can be restored.

When we die, physically, we are beyond the range of God's grace because God is consistent.

God intervened in grace while the people were trying to build the tower of Babel. He confused the languages and separated the people. This was God's way of dividing the people so they would never again get together and seek to take God's place on the earth. Our desire is to belong to something powerful so that we can gain security in our own strength but God has made us to know security in his strength.

As long as we are divided we will be more likely to rely on God's strength than on our own strength.

Chariots

During the seventies there was a book about the Chariots of the Gods[xxvi]. The thesis of this book was that advanced creatures had come from outer space and taught the people of earth how to live. The Bible actually gives the best explanation for the phenomena described in that book.

After the Lord punished the people who tried to take over the earth at Babel their languages were confused so they started to spread out and fill the earth. Each of the groups had their own language and their own share of the information that God had given to all the people when they were together. However, they were not able to communicate this information with each other.

These groups moved away and eventually filled the whole earth. They still had the desire to make a name for themselves and build a monument that reached up to heaven. All over the world people were trying to build things that were so big that they would show their own greatness[xxvii].

Christ in the Old Testament

Perhaps the New Testament is the wrong place to look for Christ in the Old Testament but it is good place to start.

Many people will argue that the Old Testament does not mention Christ at all. They say that there may be mention of someone who is coming as the promised Redeemer but that person is distinct from the Christ that we read about in the New Testament.

Some people even suggest that the Christ of the New Testament is not the same as the original Jesus of Nazareth who lived at some time around the time of Augustus Caesar. However, it is right and proper to accept the simple message of the New

Testament and to accept that the real Christ is the Jesus of Nazareth who is accurately described in the gospels[xxviii].

The Emmaus Road

After the Lord Jesus rose from the grave he met some of his followers to let them know that he was alive again, just as he had promised them[xxix].

The probable sequence of events on the resurrection morning is as follows:

The Lord Jesus was lying cold and dead in the grave but he got up a long time before it was light, as was his lifelong custom[xxx]. He left the tomb and then there was an earthquake and an angel came down and rolled the stone away from the mouth of the new tomb. Formerly there was one body in that tomb but now there was no body, just some empty grave clothes. The angel rolled the stone away to show the world that the tomb was empty. It would be very easy to say there is no body in that tomb when the tomb was closed but it is a different matter when the stone was rolled away; any one could look into the tomb and see that there was no body.

When the angel came down to roll the stone away the guards fainted with fear when they saw him and experienced the earthquake.

Mary Magdalene came to the tomb first and saw that the stone was rolled away; she thought that someone had taken his body away. She ran to tell Peter and John Christ's body was no longer in the tomb. While Mary was away telling Peter and John some other women came to the tomb; there may have been either one or two groups. These women wanted to embalm Christ's body but they didn't know how to roll the stone away. When they came to the tomb and looked inside they saw and angel and he told them that the Lord had risen from the grave.

Mary found Peter and John and told them that Christ's body wasn't there. They both ran to the tomb; John arrived first and looked in then Peter pushed past him and went into the grave. Later in the day Mary met the Lord outside the tomb.

After this the Lord met two disciples as they walked from Jerusalem to Emmaus. As they walked along the way Christ used the words of the Old Testament; "Then beginning with Moses and with all the prophets, He explained to them the things concerning Himself in all the Scriptures.[xxxi]" Christ used the Old Testament to teach these disciples all about his Incarnation, death and resurrection.

Hebrews 11

Hebrews chapter 11 gives us a roll call of some faithful men and women from the Old Testament period. Moses was one of these and we learn that Moses preferred the reproach of Christ to the riches of Egypt[xxxii]. Moses was willing to believe in the Christ who had been promised from the day that sin came into the world.

End Notes

[i] I am using ‘document’ in the sense of ‘work’ rather than a piece of paper.

[ii] The critical passages for these dates are Genesis 5: 5-32; 11: 1-32.

[iii] The modern Theory of Evolution, or Neo-Animism, is just another attempt to answer the interrogatives in a way that doesn’t include the God of the Bible. Romans 1: 18-25 explains the process that takes a person from a belief in God to the final stage where they worship God’s creatures rather than God himself.

[iv] See Exodus 2: 1-14

[v] *New American Standard Bible: 1995 update*. 1995. LaHabra, CA: The Lockman Foundation.

[vi] Damien F Mackey http://www.specialtyinterest.net/Toledoth.html <cited 12 April 2007>

[vii] http://www.newadvent.rog/cathen/04491c.htm <cited 12 April 2007>, and so for the rest of this section.

[viii] http://en.wikipedia.org/wiki/Cuneiform_script <cited 12 April 2007>, and so for the rest of this section.

[ix] K Kris Hirst http://www.archaeology.about.com/cs/educationalresour/a/history.htm <cited 12 April 2007>, and so for the rest of this section.

[x] Harris, R. L., Harris, R. L., Archer, G. L., & Waltke, B. K. (1999, c1980). *Theological Wordbook of the Old Testament* (electronic ed.) (Page 302). Chicago: Moody Press.

[xi] The Septuagint or LXX.

[xii] Psalm 115: 3; 135: 6; Isaiah 46: 10.

[xiii] This is well expressed in Genesis 1: 31.

[xiv] Exodus 33: 19 and compare Romans 9: 13.

[xv] Deuteronomy 3: 23-29

[xvi] Ruth 2: 13

[xvii] *Theological dictionary of the New Testament*. 1964-c1976. Vols. 5-9 edited by Gerhard Friedrich. Vol. 10 compiled by Ronald Pitkin. (G. Kittel, G. W. Bromiley & G. Friedrich, Ed.) (Vol. 9, Page 372-373). Grand Rapids, MI: Eerdmans.

[xviii] Young, EJ *In the Beginning,* Edinburgh: The Banner of Truth Trust, 1976, pages 22-28

[xix] Vine WE, et al, *Vine’s Expository Dictionary of Biblical Words,* Nashville: Thomas Nelson Inc, 1984, pages 96-98

[xx] http://www.ucmp.berkeley.edu/history/wegener.html <cited 11 May 2007>

[xxi] http://nobelprize.org/nobel_prizes/physics/laureates/1948/blackett-bio.html <cited 11 May 2007>
[xxii] James 4: 14
[xxiii] Ecclesiastes 9: 4
[xxiv] Rom 1: 21
[xxv] 2 Cor 12: 9-10
[xxvi] Von Däniken, Alfred *The Chariots of the Gods*, New York: Berkley, 1999
[xxvii] Genesis 11: 4
[xxviii] This is not the place to canvas this issue. You can read *Reclaiming the Bible from the Enlightened,* to pursue this further (visit www.booksthataregood.com to find out more about this book)
[xxix] Matthew 12: 40
[xxx] See Mark 1: 35
[xxxi] Luke 24:27 New American Standard Bible : 1995 update. 1995. LaHabra, CA: The Lockman Foundation
[xxxii] Hebrews 11: 26

www.ingramcontent.com/pod-product-compliance
Ingram Content Group UK Ltd.
Pitfield, Milton Keynes, MK11 3LW, UK
UKHW012230240726
13966UKWH00003B/1044

9 781847 534095